Object in Focus

C von Nolcken

The Meroë Head
of Augustus

Thorsten Opper

The British Museum

Contents

Introduction 5

The discovery of the head 8

Meroë 18

Augustus 30

Portraits and power 37

Production and provenance 47

Power and destruction 54

Summary 59

Further reading and web resources 60

Author's acknowledgements 62

Picture credits 63

Introduction

From the moment of its acquisition in June 1911, the bronze portrait head of the first Roman emperor Augustus (ruled 27 BC–AD 14) from Meroë has been considered one of the great treasures of the British Museum (fig. 1). It was chosen as one of only four Roman artworks included in the Museum's acclaimed series 'A History of the World in 100 Objects' that brought it to the renewed attention of a large audience worldwide, and it formed a key loan object in major international exhibitions that marked the 2000-year anniversary of Augustus' death in 2014.

A number of factors combine to make the Meroë Head special. First of all, it is a striking, rare survivor. Relatively few bronzes from classical antiquity have escaped the hunger of later centuries for metal that could be melted down and put to new uses. A small number of bronze portraits of Augustus are preserved, but the Meroë Head is the only one that has retained its original inlaid eyes. With their piercing, vivid gaze that forms a stark contrast to the dark green patina of the bronze surface, they lend the more than life-sized portrait head a remarkable immediacy and presence.

In addition, the head's provenance is highly unusual: for nearly two millennia it lay buried under the desert sands of northern Sudan. It is the only portrait of Augustus found in a place outside the empire that was never directly touched by Roman rule. There are inscriptions that may contain the local people's account of how this came about but they are written in ancient Meroitic, a script that we can partially decipher (one version uses Egyptian hieroglyphs) but not fully understand.

The Meroë Head's fate in antiquity provides a fascinating window into the tumultuous events of Augustus' reign and the role of portraiture in the Roman world. But first and foremost, the Meroë Head is an arresting portrait of a man who has shaped the Western world like few others. The reign of Caesar Augustus is a key part of the traditional, defining narrative of European culture that reaches from the heyday of Periclean Athens in the fifth century BC via ancient Rome to the Italian Renaissance and beyond.

Yet the Meroë Head is not only a work of art. It is testimony to the careful manipulation of his public image that turned

Augustus from a ruthless civil-war faction leader into the revered *Pater Patriae* or Father of the Fatherland, the founder of the proverbial Augustan age. While his name conjures up visions of Rome transformed from a city built in brick to one made of gleaming marble, and of the poetry of Vergil, Horace and Ovid, there is a much darker side to Augustus' reign. His successful transition from a violent upstart who overturned the old Republic in all but name, to a charismatic, autocratic ruler under a new constitutional framework, held a deep attraction for the leading protagonists of Fascist Italy and National Socialist Germany in the 1920s and 30s. This found its expression, for example, in the Fascist leader Mussolini's grand exhibition *Mostra Augustea della Romanità*, ('the Augustan Exhibition of Roman Civilization') (fig. 2), twice visited by the German *Führer* Hitler during his state visit to Italy in 1937.

Lastly, the use of ruler portraits in recent military conflicts raises important issues of historical continuity and the role of such objects in art and propaganda.

If the current interpretation of the find context is correct, then the Meroë Head was created at the very beginning of Augustus' reign, when the civil war was won and many of his great successes, but also bitter reversals and disappointments, still lay before him. In visual terms the head summed up the notion Augustus had of himself and his role in Roman society that would later find a striking expression in his political testament, the *Res Gestae* (the *Res Gestae Divi Augusti*, 'The Deeds of the Deified Augustus', gave a first-person record of Augustus' life and accomplishments and were inscribed on a number of public monuments after his death).

The circumstances of the head's rediscovery and eventual display at the British Museum form a captivating story in its own right, adding a further layer of meaning to an already complex narrative.

The Meroë Head of Augustus is an impressive monument of Roman power and yet it owes its very preservation to a rare instance of subversion of this power. It now stands as a symbol of might and defiance over the centuries.

ROMA PALAZZO DELLE ESPOSIZIONI
MOSTRA AVGVSTEA
DELLA ROMANITÀ
23 SETTEMBRE 1937 XV – 23 SETTEMBRE 1938 XVI
BIMILLENARIO DELLA NASCITA DI AVGVSTO

The discovery of the head

In the early days of December 1910, the eastern bank of
the River Nile between the Sudanese villages of Kegyek
and Deraqab, some 194 kilometres north-east of the capital
Khartoum, was a hub of human activity, crowded with
hundreds of native workers, their Arab foremen and a small
group of Europeans. A new excavation season had only just
begun at the site – the second of what would become a total
of five. It was directed by thirty-four-year-old Professor John
Garstang (1876–1956) of Liverpool University in the United
Kingdom, an ambitious and energetic man, appointed to his
newly created teaching position in 1907. His fieldwork was
financed by an organization called the Sudan Excavation
Committee. Somewhat unusually in an era of increasing
nationalism and competition between the Great Powers,
this committee was an international consortium of museum
professionals, academics and wealthy individuals, united by a
desire to partake in the thrill of archaeological adventure and a
share in the prospective finds. The museums represented were
the Musées Royaux of Brussels, the Ny Carlsberg Glyptotek in
Copenhagen and the Royal Scottish Museums in Edinburgh.
The bulk of sponsorship, however, was provided by an assorted
group of British individuals, along with the German scholar
and collector Baron von Bissingen. The eleven members of
the committee had paid in a total of £1700 towards that year's
season, with the biggest single contribution of £500 provided
by the American-born Henry Solomon Wellcome, a successful
pharmaceutics entrepreneur, but also an avid collector and
generous benefactor.

The Sudan had only relatively recently become safe again
for Western expeditions, after a prolonged insurgency that had
taken many years to suppress. In 1883, a coalition of tribes had
risen in fierce rebellion against their colonial masters. They
were led by the charismatic Muhammed Ahmed, called the
Mahdi. In the ensuing struggle, the Mahdist forces in January
1885 captured Khartoum, where they killed and beheaded
General Charles Gordon, the Governor-General of Sudan,
dealing an enormous psychological blow to the morale of
the British Empire. The Mahdi himself died later that year.

He was succeeded by Abdullahi Ibn Muhammad, also known as the Khalifa, as head of an independent Islamic state. In 1896, an Anglo-Egyptian expeditionary force under Sir Horatio Kitchener (later including a young Winston Churchill) finally began military operations against the Khalifa's forces, but only in January 1899, a little over ten years before Garstang's first campaign, was the Sudan reunited with Egypt under a British Governor-General. The brutal struggle had cost hundreds of thousands of lives, and many areas were still devastated. However, 'the pacification of the Sudan under the present administration', as Garstang drily put it in a letter to *The Times*, had now 'opened up a new field for the spade'.

The excavations covered a vast area. The River Nile was bordered here by a steep and narrow bank, rising ten metres in height, followed by a thin but very fertile strip of land, which the local villagers had turned into fields and gardens. Further east was an area of savannah, covered with substantial numbers of trees and dotted with hundreds of mounds of different sizes. At the edge of this area was a railway line, running in a southerly direction to the capital Khartoum. Beyond the railway lay the Eastern Desert. There, some four kilometres away in the distance, were two separate groups of imposing stone pyramids. This whole area, as previous finds had confirmed, was the city of Meroë, the lost capital of the ancient kingdom of Kush (see p. 18).

The first excavation season, from November 1909 to the end of February 1910, had already established some of the principal topographical features of the ancient city. The team had located and excavated in outline a monumental Temple of Ammon and some other important buildings, including a further temple. A vast necropolis (an ancient cemetery) had also been cursorily examined. During the next expedition Garstang concentrated his efforts on clearing the two temple sites, and investigating a large area, bounded in the east by a substantial wall some 300 metres long, between the river and the Temple of Ammon.

Working at astonishing speed, Garstang established that the wall formed the eastern part of a fairly regular, rectangular enclosure measuring approximately 150 by 300 metres. Roughly in axis with the temple, he found the ruins of two large, multi-roomed buildings containing finds – among them jewellery and

3 & 4. Building 'M 292' at the beginning of excavations (above) and just after the discovery of the Meroë Head (below). The Garstang Museum of Archaeology, University of Liverpool.

vessels with nuggets of gold – that suggested they might have been royal palaces. A little to the north was a further mound ('M 292', figs 3 and 4) that on excavation revealed the outlines of a square building with inner walls decorated with vivid, colourful frescoes. Horst Schliephack, Garstang's German chief assistant, photographer and draughtsman, documented these wallpaintings in a series of watercolours (figs 13a and b, to be discussed further on p. 26). In the meantime, Garstang's academic mentor, Professor Archibald Sayce, and Major Elmhurst Rhodes, a member of the excavation committee and younger brother of the famous adventurer and colonialist Cecil, had joined the party. Five days after their arrival, Garstang made an astonishing find at the mound: 'Just outside the doorway of this chamber, and buried in a clean pocket of sand (two and a half metres from the surface) there was a Roman bronze portrait head of heroic size' (figs 5 and 6). Garstang's understated remarks in his excavation report do not quite reflect the tremendous excitement he must have felt. To unearth such a splendid specimen of Roman art far from the empire's borders, deep in the Sudan, was entirely unexpected. Word about the discovery spread quickly. From Khartoum, Lord Kitchener, who

5. A Sudanese workman with the Meroë Head still in situ (or perhaps put back into its original find spot, so that the photograph could be taken). The Garstang Museum of Archaeology, University of Liverpool.

11

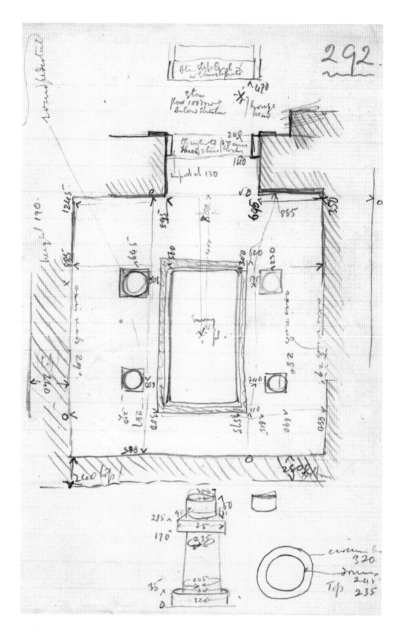

6. Garstang's sketch map of building M 292.
The find spot of the Meroë Head is marked
by an asterisk. The Garstang Museum of
Archaeology, University of Liverpool.

7. Lord Kitchener's visit to Meroë. From left to right: the Director of Railways, Lord Kitchener, Sir Francis and Lady Wingate, Professor Sayce, and John Garstang. The photograph was taken inside building M 292; parts of the ancient fresco decoration are visible behind the group (see also figs 13 and 14).

had been touring the Sudan, arrived to see the spectacular find for himself, accompanied by the Governor-General, Sir Francis Reginald Wingate and his wife (fig. 7). These were the very men who had led the re-conquest of the Sudan only a decade before.

Work at the site continued until the middle of February 1911, when the increasing heat began to make conditions uncomfortable. At any rate, Garstang must have been eager to share his exploits with the wider world. By letter, he had kept his colleagues at Liverpool abreast of events. At the end of the three-month season, 37 crates filled with finds, including the Meroë Head, were shipped from Port Sudan to England.

The British public had its first opportunity to see the bronze head when it was put on temporary display at Liverpool Museum later in May 1911. 'This head proves to be one of the finest specimens of Roman art that time has preserved to us, and Liverpool people will not fail to take advantage of a unique opportunity', a local newspaper reported in a lengthy article on the excavations. On 2 July 1911 *The New York Times* reported excitedly: 'An archaeological sensation has been created by the splendid results that have rewarded Prof. Garstang's excavations at the ancient city of Meroë in Ethiopia [. . .] the entire cost of the expedition has been defrayed by the gold discovered [. . .] chief of all the prizes is a great bronze head [. . .].' In July the head was displayed together with the other objects that had been allowed to leave the Sudan in a special exhibition in the rooms of the Society of Antiquaries at Burlington House in London, prior to a division of the finds between the members of the Excavation Committee. Patron of the exhibition was none other than Lord Kitchener himself.

Already in May, Garstang had contacted the British Museum on behalf of the Sudan Excavation Committee with a view to placing the head there. The Museum must have been delighted: only in the previous year, a magnificent full-length marble statue of Augustus had been found at the Via Labicana in Rome (fig. 17); Garstang's new discovery would provide the British Museum with a similarly impressive treasure. There had been some discussion among the members of the Excavation Committee beforehand. Valdemar Schmidt, of the Ny Carlsberg Glyptotek in Copenhagen, wrote to Garstang about the excitement the discovery had caused there and the great interest it had raised in Carl Jacobsen, the wealthy Danish industrialist, collector and founder of the Glyptotek: 'All are unanimous that every country will make great sacrifices to get the marvellous head'. Jacobsen had in fact proposed that the head should be auctioned among the members of the Committee. However, at this point Garstang revealed that the Sudan government had only allowed the head to leave the country on the condition that it should be placed in the British Museum. There followed some weeks of delicate negotiations between Garstang, Smith, and the National Art Collections Fund, a recently founded charity that aimed to

9. British World War I recruitment poster showing Lord Kitchener, the commander in chief. The poster design quickly became famous; it takes an established iconographic motif familiar from ancient Roman statues like the Prima Porta Augustus (see fig. 16) and turns it into a personal appeal of dramatic immediacy.

acquire important artworks for the nation. The Committee was most keen that the transaction should not be presented as a conventional sale, while the NACF wished to be acknowledged as the key body that had made the acquisition possible. After internal consultations, Garstang indicated that the members of the Committee were prepared to let the Museum have the head in exchange for a contribution of 1,000 Guineas (£1050 – about £60,000 in today's money) towards future excavations and a number of casts for the members of the Committee. He added that they had already received a firm offer from a Paris dealer of £5,000 and felt that with the necessary documentation it might fetch as much as £10,000. What he did not reveal, however, was that in practice, he could not actually sell to any other purchaser, as this would have violated the terms of the export licence granted in Khartoum. After a protracted exchange, the NACF finally enabled the acquisition and the head was put on display in the British Museum, where it became one of the highlights of the Bronze Room on the first floor.

Garstang's excavation at Meroë continued until 1914, when the Great War made further work impossible and the members of the excavation team and Committee suddenly found themselves on opposing sides (fig. 9). Garstang was never to resume work there or fully publish the results.

Identification

When the excavators first set their eyes on the bronze head on that auspicious December day in Meroë, they instantly recognized that they were dealing with a classical piece of sculpture, Roman, probably from the time of Augustus. Garstang and Sayce, specialists in Middle Eastern and Egyptian rather than classical art, immediately conferred by mail with their colleagues back in Liverpool and tentatively identified the head as a portrait of Germanicus, Augustus' great-nephew. A leading Roman general, Germanicus had visited Egypt on a tour of the East and inspected the border with Nubia. His portrait image, however, was mostly known through coins, with few, if any, portraits in the round securely identified.

Other experts, such as the German Professor Franz Studniczka, to whom the head was first offered for publication, and also the curators at the British Museum in London, soon proposed a different identification: it portrayed none other than Augustus, Rome's first emperor himself. The head was officially published in the excavation report of 1912 by Garstang's Liverpool colleague Robert Carr Bosanquet. As advised by Studniczka, Bosanquet provided an illuminating photographic comparison with the famous Augustus statue of Prima Porta (fig. 16) in the Vatican Museum that settled this identification beyond doubt.

Meroë

Western scholars were aware of Meroë as an almost mythical
region on the exotic fringes of the Mediterranean world,
occasionally mentioned by classical authors such as Herodotus
and Pliny. For nearly two centuries, adventurous European
travellers had been attracted by the majestic vista of numerous
tall pyramids looking out over the desert east of the city. While
they knew of Meroë from ancient texts, final proof for a positive
identification of the site had so far eluded them. The Scotsman
James Bruce (1730–1794) had embarked on an expedition
to discover the source of the Nile in 1769. On his return
journey to Egypt in 1772, he came across some ruins that he
suggested might be the remains of Meroë. The next westerner
to reach the area was the Swiss traveller and orientalist Johann
Ludwig Burckhardt (1784–1817) in 1814. Eight years later,
the Frenchman Frédéric Cailliaud (1787–1869), on a specific
mission to identify the ruins of Meroë, reached the pyramids.
His *Voyage à Méroé* of 1826 provided the first archaeological
description of the site, particularly the necropolis, accompanied
by handsome illustrations. Perhaps attracted by this, in 1834
another westerner, the Italian Guiseppe Ferlini (1800–1870)
tried to enter, and in the process partially destroyed, many of
the pyramids in search of treasure, later selling some of his
spectacular finds to the museums of Munich and Berlin. Finally,
a Prussian mission from 1842–1845, under Carl Richard
Lepsius (1810–1884), led to a more detailed investigation of
Meroitic remains and the publication of the groundbreaking
Denkmäler aus Aegypten und Aethiopien that set new standards for the
publication of archaeological sites in the field of Egyptology.

Garstang's friend and mentor, the Oxford Assyrologist
Professor Archibald Sayce, had found the area rich in material
and full of promise for further archaeological excavation: 'The
Sudan is the archaeological field of the future. The old "Island
of Meroë" is full of the sites of great cities, of temples, pyramids
and vast cemeteries entirely unexplored,' he wrote to Garstang
on 31 January 1909 after an exploratory mission to the Sudan,
ignoring earlier accounts and other recent expeditions that
already clearly heralded the beginning of a scramble for the
archaeological treasures of the region. 'Now, instead of working

at Abydos or elsewhere in Upper Egypt it would be much better worth the while of the Liverpool Institute of Archaeology to transfer its labours to the Sudan. It would be the first in the field there, and the harvest would be abundant.'

In antiquity, Meroë had been part of the powerful African kingdom of Kush, one of the oldest cultures to develop in the Nile River valley. Kush therefore had a very long and proud history. The ancient Greeks and later the Romans referred to this region as Ethiopia – not to be confused with the modern country of that name – the 'Land of the Scorched-faced People', alluding to the dark skin colour of the native population. The current name Sudan (derived from the Arabic *Bilad es-Sudan* or 'Land of the Black People') follows a similar tradition. Another commonly used term for the region is Nubia, probably derived from the Nuba tribe that rose to prominence in the medieval period.

While its borders fluctuated over the centuries, Kush's core territory extended mostly along the narrow band of the Nile from the south of modern Egypt to the north of modern Sudan, roughly between the Second and Sixth Cataracts (see fig. 12). It controlled access to the immense riches of central Africa (among them ivory, ebony, incense, precious stones and all manner of exotic animal), craved by the Egyptians, Persians and other Mediterranean powers. Other important trade routes, to the Ethiopian highlands and the Red Sea coast further east, also crossed its territory. While its geographical location made Kush a natural entrepôt for coveted trade goods, it also possessed important resources of its own, among them copper, iron, gold and precious stones. Consequently wealthy, and made up of warlike, often nomadic or semi-nomadic tribes, Kush was locked for a long period in a power struggle with Egypt to the north, each side at times gaining the upper hand. Following the withdrawal of the New Kingdom pharaohs from their Kushite territories in around 1070 BC, a powerful new state arose there with its centre at Napata in northern Sudan, below the Fourth Cataract of the Nile, in around 800 BC. Subsequently, from the late eighth to the mid seventh century BC, a strong Napatan Kushite dynasty came to rule as Pharaohs (the twenty-fifth dynasty) over Egypt in its entirety, where they left imposing monuments.

Much later, in around 270 BC, the Kushite royal burial ground was transferred from the city of Napata to Meroë. Soon after, a new dynasty was established and Meroë became the main capital.

The city was located on the eastern bank of the Nile, the centre of a wider territory bounded by the main river to the west, the Blue Nile to the south and the Atbara River to the north and east, called Butana today and 'Meroë Island' by the ancient writers. The fertile banks of the Nile here gave way to a relatively densely wooded savannah zone. Still within the rain belt, the region was home to wild animals like elephants and giraffes that today can only be found much further south. It also made possible extensive cattle herding. The abundance of wood, combined with rich deposits of iron ore, allowed for considerable iron production. Meroë itself had been settled as early as the tenth century BC. From about 590 BC onwards, it had served as an administrative centre and perhaps regional capital.

By the time of Augustus, Meroë had developed into a sizeable settlement of perhaps twenty thousand inhabitants; its culture evolved from a complex mix of indigenous Kushite traditions and external Egyptian influences. If it did not reach in size some of the cities of Roman Egypt – an unusually densely populated and highly urbanized province – it was certainly by far the largest and most monumental settlement for hundreds of miles (fig. 10).

The city was dominated by a great sanctuary of the ram-horned god Ammon, one of the key deities of the Kushite pantheon, and a number of other prominent buildings.

Built in the Egyptian style, the Temple of Ammon was an important economic as well as religious centre, reached from the east via a processional way flanked by avenues of rams, and six smaller temples that led to a monumental pylon framed by massive stone towers. Closer to the river was the 'Royal City', formerly enclosed by a strong wall on what may originally have been an island within the Nile. Its southern part was dominated by a number of large palatial-style buildings at least two storeys high, almost certainly the seat of the elite and the administration. To the north were what appear to be grand private residences, large stores and a number of smaller shrines and temples.

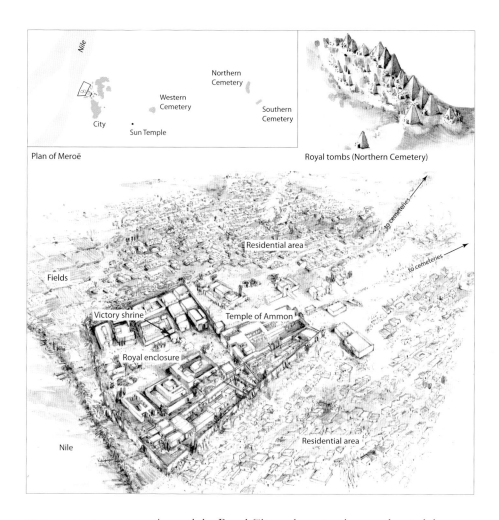

Plan of Meroë

Royal tombs (Northern Cemetery)

Labels on plan: Nile · Northern Cemetery · Western Cemetery · Southern Cemetery · City · Sun Temple

Labels on reconstruction sketch: Residential area · to cemeteries · to cemeteries · Fields · Victory shrine · Temple of Ammon · Royal enclosure · Residential area · Nile

10. Reconstruction sketch and plan of ancient Meroë. By the river is the so-called Royal enclosure, with the victory shrine (Building 'M292') at its centre.

Around the Royal City and sanctuaries were located the residential and industrial quarters, mostly made up of relatively simple dwellings of mixed type not more than one or two storeys high, combining mud-brick housing and traditional conical grass huts. Hundreds of slag heaps litter the site, hinting at abundant iron production. Further temples, larger in size, were located at the periphery. To the east followed a series of three cemeteries; the oldest located closest to the city, the other two several kilometres distant to the north and south, dominated by massive stone pyramids and their associated

21

funerary chapels, the resting places of the kings and queens of Meroë (fig. 11).

During the first century BC, the Meroites had again begun to push into Egypt, or at least into a disputed border zone, which extended from the First Cataract of the Nile to the Second (fig. 12). This stretch of territory was called the *Triakontaschoenus* or Thirty-Mile Zone. Comprised within it was a smaller area, the *Dodekaschoenus* or Twelve-Mile Zone. Both were named after the distance they extended southward, in Egyptian miles, from the traditional border at Philae on the First Cataract (*c*.315 km and *c*.126 km respectively). Effective control of this area by the Ptolemaic Greek rulers of Egypt seems to have ceased quite a while before the death of the last queen, Cleopatra, in 30 BC. Soon after Augustus' conquest of Cleopatra's realm, the people of Upper Egypt rose in rebellion, possibly supported by the Meroites. The Roman governor, Cornelius Gallus, rapidly quashed the rebellion and then confronted the ruler of Meroë. On a trilingual victory stele of 30/29 BC discovered at Philae, he claimed to have installed a ruler over the Thirty-Mile Zone, effectively annexing it to the Roman province as a new territory called *Triacontaschoenus Aethiopiae* and to have received the King of Meroë 'under his protection'. What exactly this phrase means is unclear and the different versions of the text (in Latin, Greek and Egyptian hieroglyphs) use different terminology. It may simply refer to an official treaty, but sounds almost like a client relationship, by which the ruler of Meroë had to recognize Rome as his overlord. Whatever may have been the case, in 25/24 BC the then Roman governor of Egypt, Aelius Gallus, embarked with most of his forces on an ill-fated military expedition into southern Arabia. This provided the Meroites with an opportunity for revenge. At first, the Meroitic population of the Thirty-Mile Zone may have rebelled over newly imposed Roman taxation, but it appears that they were soon joined by the Meroitic king Teriteqas at the head of his army. We are fortunate to have a brief account of these events from a well-informed source, the Greek historian and geographical writer Strabo. A near contemporary of Augustus and personal friend of Aelius Gallus, Strabo knew the area at first hand from his own travels in the entourage of the governor:

12. Map of Roman Egypt under Augustus, with the major Meroitic settlements further south along the Nile.

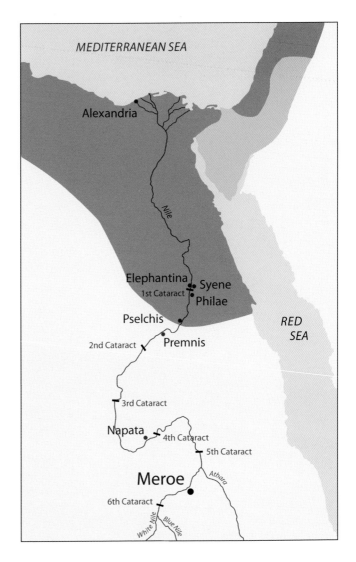

The Ethiopians, emboldened in consequence of a part of the forces in Egypt being drawn off by Aelius Gallus, who was engaged in war with the Arabs, invaded the Thebais, and attacked the garrison, consisting of three cohorts, near Syene; surprised and took Syene, Elephantina and Philae, by a sudden inroad; enslaved the inhabitants, and threw down the statues of Caesar.
(Strabo, *Geography*, Book 17, 54).

However, now the new Roman governor Gaius Petronius rushed south to confront the invaders, 'marching with less than 10,000 infantry and 800 horses against an army of 30,000 men' (ibid.). He forced the Meroites to retreat to the city of Pselchis back in their territory (a graffito by king Teriteqas was found on the walls of the local temple, marking the route of his prior advance), and began negotiations, demanding a return of the booty and an explanation for their actions.

It appears that Teriteqas was dead by then, as Petronius dealt with representatives of his queen consort Amanirenas, who succeeded him (the Meroitic title for queen was Candace, which the Romans mistook for the actual name of the queen – Strabo dramatically calls her 'a masculine woman who had lost an eye'). When these negotiations led to nothing, Petronius attacked and defeated the enemy, taking many prisoners and dispatching them to Alexandria. He then advanced further towards Napata, which was initially held by the son of the Candace, Prince Akinidad. When Akinidad fled, Petronius captured and ransacked the city, ignoring an offer from the queen to restore the prisoners and statues taken at Syene. He then withdrew back north, but not without fortifying Premnis, a natural stronghold in the centre of the Thirty-Mile Zone, and installing there a well-supplied garrison of 400 men. This fort the queen soon enough sought to attack, but she was pre-empted by Petronius' hasty return.

Further negotiations ensued, and to settle the matter once and for all, Petronius had the queen's emissaries conducted to Augustus at Samos, where he was preparing action against the Parthians. Preoccupied with this much bigger problem, Augustus quickly settled with the Meroites: 'The ambassadors obtained all that they desired, and Caesar even remitted the tribute which he had imposed' (Strabo, *Geography*, Book 17, 54). Augustus' own version of events, cited many decades later in the *Res Gestae* (see p. 6), put a rather different spin on events:

> *By my command and under my auspices two armies were led at about the same time into Aethiopia and into the Arabia called Felix, and great numbers of both enemy peoples were killed in battle and many towns were captured: In Aethiopia one came as far as the town of Napata, to which Meroë is very close.*
> (*Res Gestae Divi Augusti*, 26).

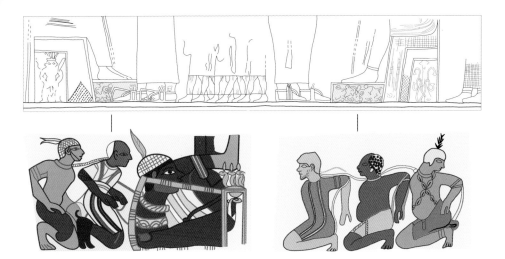

13a. (above)
Line drawing of the main wall fresco inside building M 292, the Meroitic victory shrine where the bronze head of Augustus was found.

13b. (below)
Details of the fresco showing groups of crouching prisoners (this drawing and that above are based on Horst Schliephack's 1910 watercolours).

Strabo's vivid account, echoed by similar passages in Pliny and Cassius Dio, had at first escaped Sayce's and Garstang's attention, but after the publicity surrounding the discovery of the Meroë Head, its relevance was soon pointed out. It does appear almost certain that the Meroë Head belonged to one of the plundered statues of the emperor mentioned by Strabo. The find context supports this hypothesis: the head was buried, purposefully it would seem, in a clean pocket of sand at the entrance to the shrine at Meroë. The wall paintings inside the shrine clearly show scenes of a Meroitic military triumph. These frescoes, documented in a number of Schliephack's photographs, but hard to read in detail, have now faded completely, but luckily in the 1970s a series of Schliephack's long-lost highly accurate watercolours were re-discovered in Boston. On the east wall were two large enthroned figures with sceptres, both oriented towards the centre (fig. 13a). Facing them were a standing male figure on the right and a standing female figure on the left, both at the same scale as the enthroned figures. The footstools of the two enthroned figures are ornamented with bound captives (fig. 13b). In addition, one of Schliephack's photographs of the East Wall shows a cavity filled with a human skull (fig. 14). This skull is not mentioned in the excavation reports, but these are so summary in nature that this may not mean much. If it really had originally been

14. Photograph with detail of the fresco in building M 292 during excavation. A skull is visible embedded in the wall. The Garstang Museum of Archaeology, University of Liverpool.

walled in within the shrine, this can only have happened for ritual purposes – perhaps this was the skull of a captured enemy. The building, which went through several phases, therefore appears to have served as some sort of victory shrine. The burial of the bronze head, between the steps and the door jamb, takes on a particular significance: it appears to have been placed so that every visitor to the shrine ritually trampled the face of the defeated enemy, strikingly represented by the magnificent portrait of the Roman leader, Augustus. Alternative interpretations have been advanced about the historical context – the head may have been a diplomatic gift, or perhaps it was taken some decades later from the Roman fort at Premnis, but these theories seem highly unlikely: the head is far too well preserved to have been above ground for long, and it would not normally have been left behind by Roman forces on a planned retreat. Furthermore, in 1914 Garstang discovered a small sanctuary of Ammon at Hamadab some three kilometres south of Meroë. The entrance to the structure was flanked by two large inscribed stelae with relief decoration, one of them now in the British Museum (fig. 15). The fragmentary relief band on top of this stele shows a scene not dissimilar to the fresco from the Meroë shrine: a male and female figure standing back to back, presumably the king and queen, facing two groups of attendants. Below these figures is a further relief

band showing crouching bound captives, reminiscent of the
figures on the footstools from the shrine. Among the inscriptions
the names and royal titles of the Candace Amanirenas and
Prince Akinidad can be made out. It is possible, therefore, that
this text (or that on the companion stele) gave an account of
the recent conflict with Rome from the Meroitic perspective.
Unfortunately Meroitic script, the oldest in sub-Saharan Africa,
cannot yet be properly read.

After the peace settlement at Samos, the border was
permanently established at the southern end of the Twelve-
Mile Zone. Augustus laid renewed claim to this territory by
building a large number of temples and shrines in the area
(among them the Temple of Dendur, now in the Metropolitan
Museum, New York). Trade between Rome and Meroë
continued to prosper, and many Mediterranean imports were
discovered there. The fine jewellery of Queen Amanirenas'
immediate successor, the Candace Amanishaketo, discovered
in her tomb pyramid by the adventurer Felini in the nineteenth
century, is further testimony to Meroë's wealth at the time.
There were sporadic tensions, and Pliny reports that under
Nero two Roman centurions explored Kush, as the emperor
contemplated an invasion. Only in the fourth century, when
Roman trade was channelled almost exclusively through the
Red Sea ports on the Egyptian east coast, did Meroë's power
fade and begin to be eclipsed by the Ethiopian realm at Axum.

Had Garstang already known about the circumstances
that led to the head's burial at Meroë, the site visit by Lord
Kitchener and Wingate would have appeared even more
poignant. In their struggle against the Mahdists, the Anglo-
Egyptians had fought some tribes directly descended from the
ancient peoples of Meroë, often equipped with much the same
primitive armour. And as the Meroites had ritually beheaded
the statue of Augustus, so the Mahdists had beheaded the
British commanders William Hicks and Charles Gordon two
decades before. (In turn the British later destroyed the Mahdi's
tomb and cast his bones into the Nile, Kitchener initially
retaining his skull.)

29

Augustus

Gaius Octavius or Octavian, the future Augustus, was born on 23 September 63 BC. He owed his astonishing rise to eminence to an unerring instinct for power and its finer mechanics, and an ability to engage the main interest groups within Roman society – the knights, the military and the urban plebs – at a time of enormous social change and political upheaval. For decades, the institutions of the old Republic had been overwhelmed by Rome's vast expansion, which brought enormous wealth for a few and poverty for the masses, and intense rivalry between the leading aristocrats and military commanders at the expense of the common good.

Augustus' paternal ancestors came from the town of Velitrae near Rome and were members of the order of knights. His father had been the first in the family to reach a position of some eminence in the capital and enter the senate. After his father's tragic early death, the four-year-old boy's maternal relatives came to the fore: his mother Atia was the daughter of Julia, sister of Gaius Julius Caesar. The Julii were one of the great patrician families of Rome and through Caesar were prominently back in the public eye. Over the next fifteen years, Caesar consolidated his power and eventually achieved quasi monarchical rule as *dictator perpetuus* ('dictator in perpetuity') after a brutal civil war.

Octavius was outside Italy to complete his studies, when the life-changing news reached him of Caesar's assassination by a group of disaffected senators on 15 March 44 BC. He immediately returned home. Gathering around him some of Caesar's loyal troops, he took the momentous decision to claim leadership of the Caesarian faction, avenge Caesar's death and look after the interests of his family and allies by any means necessary. In the famous account of his life and achievements, the *Res Gestae*, he later put it thus: 'Aged nineteen, by my own decision and at my own expense, I raised an army with which I freed the Republic oppressed by the tyranny of one faction' (*Res Gestae Divi Augusti*, 1). On 6 May, he reached the capital and formally accepted Caesar's legacy, who had adopted him in his will. His name from now on was Gaius Julius Caesar Octavianus. The Caesarian faction was not unified. Octavian's main rival was Marcus Antonius (83–30 BC), a powerful character and gifted public speaker. Octavian, however, gained a following by faithfully executing the terms of Caesar's will, including a cash gift for every member of the urban plebs and lavish games. During these games a comet appeared, which was immediately declared a sign that Caesar had become a god. Octavian would from now on use the comet as a potent symbol and adopt the name *Imperator Caesar Divi Filius* ('Son of the Deified').

The senate admitted the nineteen-year-old to its ranks and gave him an official military command against the by now openly rebellious Antony, which he took on 7 January 43 BC. The senate's forces defeated Antony in a major battle at Mutina in northern Italy, but both consuls died in the fighting. Octavian took over their legions and marched on Rome, where he induced the senate to appoint him consul on 19 August 43 BC. Yet in the meantime, the senate had also recognized Caesar's leading assassins, Marcus Iunius Brutus (85–42 BC) and Gaius Cassius (85–42 BC), who had seized the provinces of Macedonia and Syria. Faced with this threat, the divided Caesarians reconciled their differences. Octavian, Marc Antony and Aemilius Lepidus (*c*.89–12 BC) formed an alliance, having themselves appointed by popular vote *tresviri rei publici constituendae* ('triumvirs to set the Republic in order'), to uphold constitutional legitimacy. They re-introduced the system of proscriptions, declaring their opponents enemies of the state and confiscating their property. Entire families of the old Republican elite were wiped out, to be replaced by the triumvirs' followers. At the Battle of Philippi in Macedon in October 42 BC, the Caesarians decisively defeated their Republican opponents and divided the provinces between them.

Following further battles, Octavian became sole ruler of the West in 36 BC. Antony, by contrast, suffered a serious defeat against the Parthians, Rome's great rivals in the East, and turned to the Queen of Egypt, who had become his lover, for military support. Perceiving this alliance as a threat to the Roman Republic, the senate declared war, nominally not on Antony but on Cleopatra. The inhabitants of Italy and the Western provinces swore their loyalty to Octavian, who from now on claimed to act by 'universal consensus'.

In September 31 BC, the opponents' naval forces met at

Actium, in north-western Greece. Octavian's fleet won the day. Defeated, Antony fled with Cleopatra to Egypt.

The Battle of Actium subsequently became the foundation myth of the new order, endlessly celebrated as a victory of Rome and the West over her Eastern adversaries, and all achieved under Octavian's leadership. Octavian pursued Antony into Egypt, defeating his forces in a battle near Alexandria in August 30 BC, after which both Antony and Cleopatra committed suicide. Octavian had achieved final victory.

Egypt, until then an independent Hellenistic kingdom, became a Roman province. Immense booty, coupled with the rich revenue of the new province, allowed Octavian a lavish victory celebration with a spectacular triple triumph in 29 BC. He officially closed the doors of the Temple of Janus, a symbolic act (the doors were open in times of conflict and closed in times of peace) ending a period of near constant war that had begun with Caesar's crossing of the Rubicon twenty years earlier. The empire was tired, the elite decimated.

Octavian now had to maintain and consolidate his sole power while avoiding the outright monarchical model that had so clearly failed Caesar. The solution was a nominal return to the institutions of the old Republic – as he had promised all along – while he secured his status through the accumulation of traditional offices and legal competencies. The public mood, with people yearning for peace and stability after decades of strife, was clearly favourable.

In January 27 BC, Octavian formally handed supreme power back to the senate and people of Rome. However, he remained in office as consul and kept personal control of key border provinces, in which most of the army was concentrated, and gradually transformed the military into a professional, standing force personally loyal to him. Combined with his vast financial resources and network of faithful supporters, this gave him immense power and authority.

In return for this nominal restoration of the Republic, the senate voted new honours for Octavian. A golden shield inscribed with his four cardinal virtues (valour, clemency, justice and piety) was put up in the senate house, and he was awarded a civic crown for having rescued the citizens. Both the shield and crown became much-used symbols of the new regime.

In addition, Octavian was given the new name Augustus, the Illustrious. This title was unique to him and carried a wide array of meanings, even touching on the religious. From now on, he styled himself *Imperator* (Emperor) *Caesar Augustus*. Under his successors, this collection of names would become the official imperial title. Augustus now acted as *princeps*, the first man of the state. The practical running of these arrangements would be fine-tuned over the coming decades.

His rule consolidated, Augustus set about the transformation of Rome. In 17 BC, he officially celebrated the *ludi saeculares* (secular games), traditionally meant to inaugurate a new era and ritually renew the community, accompanied by Horace's tribute hymn, *Carmen Saeculare* ('Song of the Ages'). His own house on the Palatine remained relatively modest, but took on more and more of an official character. One area was turned into a sacred precinct for the god Apollo, with a temple built entirely of marble, the first in Rome. In the forum, one of Augustus' very first measures was to build a temple for the deified Caesar. After the Battle of Actium, he also erected a new speaker's platform in front of it, decorated with the prows of the captured enemy ships. The Basilica Julia, an imposing public building housing law courts, offices and shops had been begun by Caesar and was now completed. Opposite, Augustus built the Curia Julia, which linked through to the Forum of Caesar. Next to this, and financed from the spoils of war, he then built his own monumental forum. It was dominated by a temple to Mars Ultor, the Avenger, since Augustus had vowed to avenge Caesar's death before the Battle of Philippi. Portrait galleries on either side showed great leaders of Roman history beginning with Romulus (one of the mythical founders of Rome) and members of the Julian family, going all the way back to their mythical ancestor Aeneas. Rome's history and that of Augustus' family were thus firmly integrated. With Augustus as the leader, both came fortuitously together. Ample space was devoted in the *Res Gestae* to these architectural endeavours, and in one year alone Augustus claimed to have renovated 82 temples. In sum, he appeared as a new founder of the city, a second Romulus. He showed similar generosity in the provinces, and saw many of them for himself on extended travels. While he

17. Marble portrait statue of Augustus, just over life-size, from the Via Labicana in Rome. Augustus is shown as officiating priest, his toga drawn up over his head. Late 1st century AD. Museo Nazionale Romano, Palazzo Massimo alle Terme inv. no. 56230.

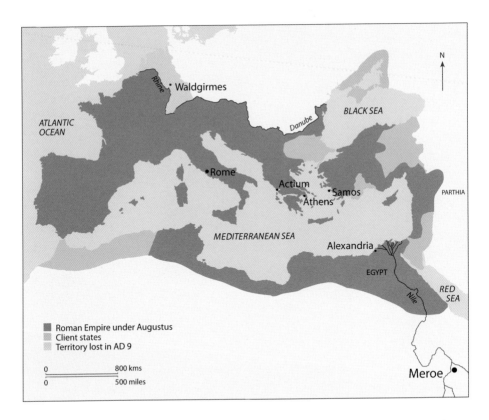

18. Map of the Roman Empire under Augustus.

suffered a number of military setbacks, Augustus conquered vast territories and established allied principalities around the periphery of the empire (fig. 18). Statues of Augustus (such as those shown in figs 16 and 17) were erected throughout the empire, their purpose to serve as a continuous reminder of the power of Rome and its emperor. At his death in AD 14, he was succeeded by his stepson Tiberius, whom he had adopted after the premature death of his other designated heirs.

Portraits and power

Honorific portrait statues were a key currency in the constant
struggle for prestige that preoccupied the traditional elites of
ancient society – in the Greek city states of the classical period
and the kingdoms that were established by the successors of
Alexander the Great (356–323 BC) in what is known as the
Hellenistic period, as well as in Rome. Initially in Greece,
portraits that were likenesses of living persons were exceedingly
rare. Such statues at first were highly idealized, and individuality
was only conveyed through the inscribed name on the base.
This gradually changed during the course of the later fifth and
fourth centuries BC. The process accelerated under autocratic
rulers such as the kings of Macedon, who could in part draw
on Eastern traditions. Greek artists soon developed a specific
vocabulary to capture the essence of Hellenistic kingship,
stressing the god-like heroic qualities and dynamic power of
the subject. The Romans had their own portrait tradition
that valued different aspects, particularly a natural-looking
face. This may have been influenced by a tradition within the
families of high-ranking Roman nobles to keep wax masks of
their ancestors on display in their houses. These masks were
also worn by actors in funeral processions, as the Greek writer
Polybius tells us, so that the prominent line of important family
clans was visible to all. Realism and the marks of maturity and
advanced age thus became prized elements of Roman portraits.
Strikingly naturalistic styles had also been developed by Greek
artists during the Hellenistic period. While in the Greek world
these were not so much used for portrait statues but rather
for representations of genre figures and low-life characters,
it was this mode of representation that was chosen by Roman
clients commissioning Greek artists for their portraits. The
increasing hold of Greek artistic traditions over Rome led to
some conflict in the mid-Republic. Portrait statues in the new
style often combined idealized Greek bodies with naturalistic
Roman heads, creating peculiar hybrids. Nudity in itself was
an unfamiliar concept to the Romans in the public sphere and
portrait statues had traditionally shown the honoured person
in civic or military dress. As time went by, the leading generals

of the late Republic adopted more and more of the elements of Hellenistic ruler iconography. Their new portrait styles in a sense undermined time-honoured Republican traditions just as much as their policies.

A portrait statue consisted of a number of complementary elements that each conveyed an important message. Firstly, there was a recognizable portrait head. Then there was the full-length body, usually draped in an appropriate civic or military costume but occasionally nude. Finally, there was a dedicatory inscription, carved into a tall, decorative base that raised the statue to an imposing height. The inscription gave the name of the person honoured, his or her main achievements, such as important offices held, and the reason for the dedication of the statue, as well as the identity of the person or administrative body that had dedicated it and paid for it.

The specific format of the statue and the material it was made of were further indicators in the finely nuanced system of visual markers that reflected the honoured person's status. Most statues depicted the portrayed standing upright; a seated statue expressed higher rank, while the pinnacle was a statue on horseback. Later, this could be topped by statues of victorious generals in their triumphal chariots. The majority of statues displayed in public squares were made of bronze; marble statues were also numerous, but slightly less prestigious and otherwise more common in architectural contexts. Most impressively, there were statues made of gold and silver (or at least gilded or silvered bronze).

Finally, the location in which a statue was set up mattered greatly. In the public sphere, statue dedications were strictly regulated and had to be approved by civic authorities that also allocated a specific position for the monument. A location in a much frequented public square, next to an important building, was naturally more sought after than a dedication in a more remote spot. Inevitably, this could lead to an immense overcrowding of certain areas with hundreds of statues and ever more extravagant monuments.

It is against the background of this world of competing images that we need to judge the portraits of Augustus.

The portraits of Augustus

The promotion of his public image was of greatest concern to Augustus from the very beginning of his political career, when (in the words of his rival Marc Antony) he was still only 'a boy who owed everything to his name' – the name of his adoptive father, Julius Caesar. His portraits put a face to the name, and in the persistent struggle between rival political factions, they served as potent symbols and rallying points for his supporters.

More sculptured portraits are preserved of Augustus than of any other Roman emperor – the latest comprehensive scholarly catalogue lists some 210 versions made of bronze and marble. There are a number of obvious reasons for the popularity of Augustus' image: he held power over a long period of time and successfully established a dynasty in which members of his own family succeeded him, so that his statues were still produced in later reigns for inclusion in dynastic groups. First and foremost, however, Augustus had an instinctive grasp of the importance of portraits as powerful propagandistic tools in the political struggle for power and the manipulation of his public perception. Later, after the years of bloody factional strife, these portraits became a means for people all over the exhausted empire to show their loyalty to the new order and its founder. Augustus thus established a precedent that all later emperors would follow. In terms of the history and development of Roman portraiture as an artistic genre, what we see during Augustus' reign are the very beginnings of a complex system which ensured that centrally designed portrait types were disseminated widely throughout the empire and copied mechanically in local workshops.

It is a complex task to make sense of this wealth of material. Surviving portraits are divided into different types. None of the original models on which these types must have been based have survived, but they can be at least partially reconstructed through a careful comparison of the appearance and style that certain related copies share. Based on various stylistic criteria and technical characteristics, as well as external evidence, such as inscribed coins, a date is determined for the creation of the prototype and the individual replicas. Finally, attempts can be made to identify the occasions (important political events, anniversaries, succession arrangements etc) for which these

types were created. By applying these criteria, the mass of Augustus' portraits can be very broadly divided into three main types, sometimes named after what used to be considered the best replicas (fig. 19).

Type I ('Alcudia', figs 19a–b) was created for Augustus' first images and remained in use throughout the period of the triumvirate and civil war. It was a masterful adaptation of the standard iconographic vocabulary used for ruler portraits in the Greek kingdoms of the East – the traditional language of power – to specific Roman concerns. This made it modern, easily recognizable and individual, ensuring its success in the streets. Visual formulae that could be associated with power, dynamism and leadership were the emphatic turn of the head, the contracted brows and furrowed forehead and the big, voluminous mass of hair. These contrasted with a long neck and a lean, bony face, perhaps reflecting elements of the young Augustus' real appearance. The small mouth with thin lips and the high, sharp cheekbones create an impression of determined asceticism and draw attention to the eyes. Here we have a self-effacing, youthful and charismatic leader. Coins show this type in use in the 30s BC. There may have been two closely related versions, perhaps short-lived predecessor types, of which there are only a very small number of surviving replicas.

Type II ('Forbes', figs 19c–d) is relatively close to Type I in appearance. The main differences are a much simpler, flatter arrangement of the hair, especially above the forehead, where it appears simply brushed to the right, and a somewhat smoother, more harmoniously proportioned face. This type was prominently used on an important state monument, the *Ara Pacis* or Altar of Peace that was voted in 13 BC and completed in 9 BC. However, the type may originally have been created to celebrate the final end of the civil wars, perhaps on the occasion of Octavian's triple triumph in 29 BC. It essentially toned down the emphatic style of the earlier portrait and showed Augustus less youthful.

Type III ('Prima Porta', figs 19e–f) finally abandoned this tradition altogether, taking inspiration from a much earlier period: the high classicism of the fifth century BC. Here can be seen the influence of iconic masterpieces of Greek art such as the Doryphoros by the celebrated sculptor Polycleitus (fig. 20). This type, to which the Meroë Head belongs, was by far the most popular of Augustus' portrait types: almost two and a half times the number of replicas are preserved for this type than all other types put together. Type III created a timeless image, far removed from contemporary styles and above contemporary politics. It is usually called the Prima Porta type, after the find-spot of the finest replica (see fig. 16). Its hallmarks are a distinctive, yet simple and easily recognizable lock pattern above the forehead and a calm, classical rather than individualistic-looking physiognomy. In all likelihood, this type was created in about 27 BC when Augustus received his new name from the senate. It remained in use throughout his reign, the ageless features of the face never altered or updated.

The exact date for the creation of these portrait types and the relative chronological sequence of types II and III in particular are not easy to establish and, in this case, coins are not as reliable a help as one could hope for. Dating the types is also difficult because the creation of a new portrait type did not mean that the older versions ceased to be copied, and so different types could be used in parallel, and sometimes older types were updated to include elements of newer ones.

The Meroë Head appears to be a very close copy of type III, faithfully reproducing its distinctive features (and its find context has been used as a further argument for the early date of the type). However, in difference to other replicas, perhaps reflecting a particular workshop tradition, the corners of the mouth turn downwards.

Augustus' portraits also became the template for the images of his intended successors (e.g. Marcellus, Gaius and Lucius Caesar). In the past, such portraits have been confused with representations of Augustus himself, as a young man. However, there is no evidence that such early portraits of Augustus ever existed, and it is obvious from the clear, formal dependency of these types on images of the mature emperor that they were created later for younger members of the imperial family.

Contemporary Roman texts, inscriptions and coins give us a glimpse of the contexts in which these images were used. As far as we know, the first public statue was voted for Augustus on 2 January 43 BC. It was a gilded statue on horseback that was set up on or near the *rostrae*, the famous speaker's platform in the *Forum Romanum*. The statue commemorated the nineteen-

20. Roman marble version of the Doryphoros, after a fifth-century BC bronze statue by the sculptor Polycleitus. c.120–50 BC. Height 198.12 cm. Minneapolis Institute of Arts, inv. 86.6.

21a–c. Denarii of 31 BC with statues of Octavian: Octavian on horseback (right); Octavian holding a lance and a ship's prow, his right foot resting on a globe (far right); statue of Octavian on a *columna rostrata*, a column decorated with the prows of captured enemy ships (below). British Museum R.6011, R.6162 and R.6168.

year-old Octavian's settlement with the senate and visibly established him as a key player at the heart of Roman politics. So important was the propagandistic value of this image, that it was immediately represented on coins issued by Octavian's supporters – even before the actual monument had been produced (fig. 21a).

Two other important statues, known from representations on coins and in literary sources, were dedicated to Octavian after his naval victories over his civil-war rival Sextus Pompeius. One represented him in the pose of Neptune, god of the sea, his right foot on a globe, a lance in his left hand and a ship's ornament in his right (fig. 21b). The other showed him standing on a column decorated with ships' prows (fig. 21c). The symbolic potency and practical power of these highly partisan images was such that followers of the competing political factions regularly pulled down the statues of their adversaries.

After the victory at Actium, many of these images – provocative, consciously divisive and now in a sense unnecessary – were withdrawn from circulation. This was an important gesture in itself, and Augustus thought it worth an explicit mention in his *Res Gestae*:

> About eighty silver statues of me on foot or on horse or in chariots had been set up in the city [of Rome], *which I myself removed and with the money from them I set up golden offerings in the Temple of Apollo in my name and in the names of those who had honoured me with the statues.* (*Res Gestae Divi Augusti*, 24).

The new portrait types provided a clear break with the past and stood for a new beginning in the unified empire under Augustus' leadership. In particular type III, the Prima Porta type, must have been considered so successful in symbolizing these values that it remained unchanged for forty years. It is illuminating to compare these carefully constructed images with descriptions of Augustus' real appearance. The first-century AD writer Suetonius gives the following account in his biography *De vita Caesarum*, commonly known as 'The Twelve Caesars':

> He was unusually handsome and exceedingly graceful at all periods of his life, though he cared nothing for personal adornment. He was so far from being particular about the dressing of his hair, that he would have several barbers working in a hurry at the same time, and as for his beard he now had it clipped and now shaved, while at the very same time he would either be reading or writing something. His expression, whether in conversation or when he was silent, was [. . .] calm and mild [. . .]. He had clear, bright eyes, in which he liked to have it thought that there was a kind of divine power, and it greatly pleased him, whenever he looked keenly at anyone, if he let his face fall as if before the radiance of the sun; but in his old age he could not see very well with his left eye. His teeth were wide apart, small, and ill-kept; his hair was slightly curly and inclining to golden; his eyebrows met. His ears were of moderate size, and his nose projected a little at the top and then bent slightly inward. His complexion was between dark and fair. He was short of stature [. . .], but this was concealed by the fine proportion and symmetry of his figure [. . .].
> (Suetonius, *Life of Augustus*, 79.1–2).

Of course, the purpose of Suetonius' text may be to sketch a suitable character portrait of Augustus rather than present a description of his appearance strictly based on facts. What is interesting, however, is his focus on Augustus' large eyes and the power he ascribed to them. This is echoed by other writers, and a feature recognizable on some (but not all) of the surviving portrait sculptures, and notably the Meroë Head. Large eyes, usually with the gaze turned upwards to the heavens, had already been a characteristic of Hellenistic ruler portraits in the wake of Alexander the Great, stressing their heroic quality and constant communion with the gods. Augustus, too, appears as a charismatic leader of men, his all-seeing eyes adding life to his otherwise calm and authoritative countenance.

Production and provenance

The production of a larger than life-sized bronze statue of the quality of the Meroë Augustus required considerable skill and experience, as well as access to reliable models of the official portrait type. None of these could have been readily available in southern Egypt, and it is therefore highly likely that the statue was imported from elsewhere. Two places in particular come to mind and have been suggested in the past: Rome itself, or Alexandria – the capital of Roman Egypt, the second most populous city of the empire and an important artistic centre in its own right. Later papyri confirm that Alexandrian workshops did indeed supply towns in Upper Egypt with bronze statuary.

There is a small and peculiar detail in the coiffure of the Meroë Head that could possibly hint at an Eastern provenance: the lock of hair that reaches down from the temple in front of the left ear does not fall in a uniform way. While most strands curve forward towards the face, the strand furthest to the right moves in the opposite direction, towards the ear. This seemingly unimportant motif is only shared by a very small number of other replicas of the Prima Porta type (figs 16, 19e–f). Of these ten or so replicas, three apparently come from Egypt and three others are in basalt or granite, local materials used by many Egyptian workshops. Perhaps this gives more weight to a possible Alexandrian origin of the Meroë Head, but ultimately, the question of where it was produced will have to remain open.

The Meroë Head is made of bronze, a term archaeologists use as equivalent to the ancient terms $\chi\alpha\lambda\varkappa\delta\varsigma$ in Greek or *cuprum* in Latin to denote any type of copper alloy. According to an analysis carried out by British Museum scientists, the specific alloy used for the Meroë Head contained 72 % copper, 22.6 % lead, 5.45 % tin, 0.7 % zinc, 0.035 % nickel, 0.022 % silver, as well as small traces of iron and antimony.

The Meroë Head was produced in the so-called indirect lost wax technique (fig. 22). The lower rim of the neck corresponds to the edge of the original cast, so the head was made separately from the body to which it was later joined. From the original model (fig. 22.1), perhaps a plaster cast that had been sent from a metropolitan workshop, the sculptor and his assistants took a number of interlocking sectional piece-moulds. These piece-

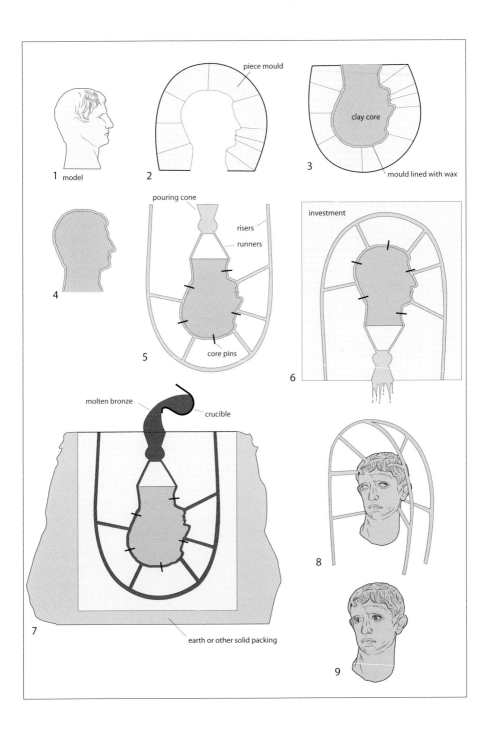

1 model

2 piece mould

3 clay core — mould lined with wax

4

5 pouring cone — risers — runners — core pins

6 investment

7 molten bronze — crucible — earth or other solid packing

8

9

22. The major stages
of the casting process,
from mould-making to
finished product.

moulds were most likely made of clay or plaster. When locked together, they retained an exact negative image of the model (22.2). Next, the bronze casters lined the mould with liquid wax. Then, they filled the lined mould with a core of clay (22.3). Once the core hardened, they could remove the piece-mould and make some final changes to the outer wax surface (22.4). It is possible that the Meroë Head at this stage was briefly rested on the back of the crown, since this appears slightly flattened.

The Meroë Head's ears are solid, indicating that the sculptor modelled them freely in wax and only added them at this point, perhaps to facilitate the previous process of creating the piece-moulds. At this stage, other little details could be corrected or added in the wax. Next, a series of runners and risers were modelled in wax and connected to the surface of the head (22.5). Runners are the channels through which the bronze would later be poured into the mould, while risers allow the air and gases trapped within it to escape safely. Once these had been added, the bronze-caster would drive a number of long, square metal pins through the wax and into the clay core. Then, he could construct a so-called 'investment mould' around the wax structures. This was made of clay, and able to withstand the heat of the molten metal when it was poured into the mould. The metal pins, projecting several centimetres from the surface of the wax model, were firmly embedded in the investment mould, so that they could hold all the separate elements firmly in place (22.6).

In the final stage before the actual casting process, the mould would be heated in order to melt out the wax, creating a cavity between the investment mould and the clay core. Finally, the metal could be poured into the mould (22.7). To the bronze caster and his assistants, this was the most tense and uncertain moment; the stresses on the mould were considerable and much could go wrong with the cast. Fortunately, with the indirect casting method the original model stayed intact, so that in the worst case the process could be repeated until a satisfactory outcome was achieved.

Once the bronze had cooled down, the workers could dismantle the investment mould and reveal the new head. Now began the most labour-intensive part of the production process that would determine the final appearance of the cast.

The runners and risers, as well as the pins, had to be carefully removed and the points where they had been connected to the surface of the head smoothed down (22.8).

Little pockets of air or gas left in the mould during the casting process could cause holes in the bronze, which now had to be patched up. For this purpose, the area around the hole was cut out with a special tool to form a rectangular cavity that could then be filled with a repair patch of the same shape. When the surface was polished, these patches were hardly visible. The Meroë Head shows very few evident traces of such repairs, indicating the good quality of the cast, although the surface corrosion (red cupride and green malachite) now effectively hides any blemishes. X-Ray images of the head do show, however, quite a number of impurities in the bronze, particularly in the profile views, although happily, these mostly did not appear on the surface, except for a small circular hole on the left side of the neck near the bottom (fig. 23). Also visible are the square remains of the metal pins that fixed the position of the clay core within the investment mould. Closer examination also reveals the outline of a few repair patches, for example on the neck below the chin. The fact that these patches have not fallen out, as on so many other ancient bronzes, is confirmation that the head cannot have been on display for a long time between its production and burial at Meroë.

Finally, last details were incised with fine chisels, in this case the individual strands of hair that characterize the plastically rendered locks of the coiffure and the eyebrows. Then the surface would be finely polished to sparkle with a golden sheen.

Particular care was taken with the eyes, small masterpieces in themselves (often made by specialist craftsmen called *fabri oculariūi*, 'eye makers'): the eyeballs, made of highly polished white limestone, were cut into a wedge shape and inserted separately with thin, serrated sheets of copper or bronze for the eyelashes. Traces of these are still visible on the Meroë Head, although the lashes themselves have broken off. Irises, made out of a green glass paste, and pupils made out of nearly black paste, each encircled by a narrow copper ring, were then set into the limestone. The tear ducts were indicated with reddish glass paste. Together, these elements gave the eyes a strikingly lifelike effect. The lips, by contrast, were not rendered separately.

23. X-ray photographs of the Meroë Head. Minor impurities in the metal and the outlines of square repair patches are visible. British Museum.

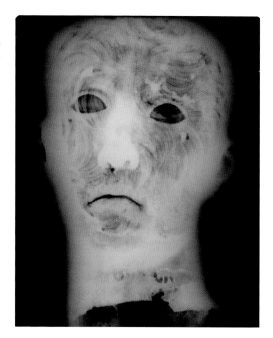

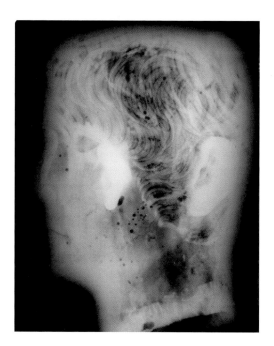

24. The main views of
the Meroë Head.

On many other bronzes, they were made of small copper sheets, giving a lifelike reddish colour; it is possible, however, that they may have been painted on the Meroë Head.

It is clear that the Meroë Head (fig. 24) originally formed part of a full-length statue that was assembled from several separately cast pieces. This statue would have been draped rather than nude, so that the garment or body armour would hide the joins between the different parts. We do not know what this statue looked like and whether it showed Augustus in civilian or military costume, seated, standing or on horseback. Perhaps in a frontier settlement or military installation a statue in military dress would have seemed most appropriate. The slight inclination and marked turn of the head to the right at any rate are very close to the marble Prima Porta statue (fig. 16) that showed Augustus in full body armour on foot, addressing his troops.

Power and destruction

If the Kushite incursion into southern Egypt that led to the capture of the Meroë Head was a relatively minor incident, then Augustus suffered a much more severe setback some thirty years later, towards the end of his reign. In AD 9, Germanic war bands under the overall leadership of Arminius, a noble of the Cherusci tribe, ambushed and annihilated three Roman legions and their associated auxiliary units under the command of Publius Quinctilius Varus, in the vast Teutoburg Forest. Varus' corpse was mutilated, his head passed between tribal leaders and eventually sent on to Augustus in Rome. A trusted and experienced professional who was married to one of Augustus' great nieces and had been in the emperor's entourage when the Meroitic envoys had come to Samos in 21 BC, Varus had been tasked with transforming the tribal territories between the river Rhine and the river Elbe, hitherto linked to Rome through an improvised system of separate treaties and individual allegiances, into a fully-fledged Roman province. Recent archaeological discoveries have revealed for the first time how far Roman measures to provide a basic infrastructure for the projected new province had in fact advanced. Excavations at Waldgirmes in the Lahn River Valley, for example, have brought to light a small Roman town.

Built from scratch by the Roman military, the settlement appears to have served as a small trading and production centre and may have been part of a series of proto-urban nuclei planted in the new territories. Although in use for a short period of only fifteen years or so, the town had been given a forum that included an official assembly hall providing administrative and religious facilities next to an open square surrounded by colonnades. A series of statue bases were found in the centre of the square. Most remarkably, scattered throughout the site, archaeologists also discovered fragments of a gilded bronze statue of Augustus on horseback. It appears that the settlement came to a violent end in the immediate aftermath of the Varus battle. The statue was hacked to pieces. The most significant fragment so far, the front part of the horse's head with remains of its ornate trappings, was discovered in a well, where it may have been ritually deposited by the triumphant Germanic tribesmen (fig. 25).

25. Fragments of an equestrian bronze statue of Augustus from Waldgirmes, Germany. Römisch-Germanische Kommission.

26. Toppling of a colossal bronze statue of Saddam Hussein, Baghdad.

The parallels to the events surrounding the Meroë Head are striking and once more attest the great symbolic significance accorded to the imperial image on both sides. From the deserts of southern Egypt to the wild forests of central Europe, the Romans made every effort quickly to supply even the far-flung outposts of their empire with statues of the emperor. The image stood in for the person of the ruler. Unsurprisingly, such images were therefore a prime target for the empire's enemies.

While such concepts and practices may at first seem remote to our experience today, on closer scrutiny, the potent symbolism of such acts is still being used in the political sphere, now multiplied through modern mass media. Immediately on their capture of Baghdad during the Second Gulf War in 2003, American troops pulled down a colossal bronze statue of the defeated Iraqi leader Saddam Hussein (figs 26, 27). Presented as a spontaneous action by the newly liberated Iraqis, but in fact carefully planned and logistically supported by the US

military, the event was widely covered by the media and of
such tremendous symbolic power that it was shown on all news
bulletins worldwide. In part, this may also have been a symbolic
act of revenge, for after the First Gulf War, a floor mosaic with
the portrait of the American president George Bush Senior
had been installed at the entrance of the Al-Rashid hotel in
Baghdad (fig. 28). All visitors to the hotel, particularly western
politicians and businessmen who used to stay there, were
accordingly forced ritually to trample the face of the leader of
the biggest power in the West – just as the Meroites did with the
face of Augustus outside their victory shrine 2000 years earlier.

The comparison with the portraits of Saddam Hussein also
brings us much closer to the original context of the Meroë
Head. It was not conceived as a work of art, even if it has
taken on that quality to us today, but as a raw symbol of
power, copied mechanically and centrally distributed.

28. Floor mosaic of President George Bush Senior outside a hotel in Baghdad. Following the occupation of the city, the mosaic was immediately removed by American troops.

Summary

The Meroë Head combines in one object many different stories. It gives a glimpse of how Augustus, the most powerful man in the Roman Empire, wished to be seen by his own people and by foreigners alike, even in the most far-flung corners of the Roman world, and how a highly efficient system evolved that combined artistic skill and technical competence in the production and dissemination of portrait sculpture to make this possible.

The bronze also reflects a history of conflict in Africa between local and outside powers, from antiquity to the modern era, that includes highly evocative incidences of symbolic and all too real beheadings designed to make strong public statements. Almost by accident, it has become an ambiguous symbol of power and resistance at the same time.

The discovery of the head offers a poignant example of international scholarly cooperation and its very fragility on the eve of the Great War. After the outbreak of hostilities, John Garstang became an ambulance driver on the Western Front, his British assistant Robert Elcum Horsefall fell near Cambrai in northern France, and his German Assistant Horst Schliephack fought for the Central Powers in the Caucasus, the region at the border of Europe and Asia, situated between the Black and the Caspian seas. If, as a consequence, the documentation of the Meroë excavations by modern standards leaves much to be desired, the rich photographic record preserved in the Garstang Museum of Archaeology, in the University of Liverpool offers some compensation and forms an extremely interesting body of material in its own right.

Finally, just as the Meroë Head was intended as an embodiment of political power, the manipulation of ancient history and art for political purposes in the modern era is increasingly becoming the focus of both scholarly and popular attention. With all these layers of interpretation and meaning, the Meroë Head has lost none of its power to fascinate.

Further reading and web resources

The following titles provide a good overview of the main aspects touched upon in this book and will list more specialist scholarly articles in their bibliographies.

Augustus in history and art

D. Boschung, *Die Bildnisse des Augustus* (Berlin 1993)

W. Eck, *The Age of Augustus* (2nd edn, Oxford 2007)

D. E. L. Haynes, 'The date of the bronze head of Augustus from Meroë', in *Alessandria e il Mondo Ellenisticoromano: Studi in Onore di Achille Adriani* (Rome 1983), pp. 177–181, pls 31–33

G. Lahusen and E. Formigli, *Römische Bildnisse aus Bronze: Kunst und Technik* (Munich 2001), 58–60, no. 18

E. La Rocca et al (eds), *Augusto* (exhibition catalogue, Milan 2013). French edition: *Auguste* (exhibition catalogue, Paris 2014)

N. MacGregor, *A History of the World in 100 Objects* (London 2010), pp. 221–226

Paul Zanker, *The Power of Images in the Age of Augustus* (Michigan 1990)

Meroë and Meroitic culture

M. Baud (et al.), *Meroë: un empire sur le Nil* (exhibition catalogue, Paris 2010)

J. Garstang, *Meroë: The City of the Ethiopians* (London 1911)

L. Török, *The Kingdom of Kush: Handbook of the Napatan-Meroitic Civilization* (Leiden 1997)

D. A. Welsby, *The Kingdom of Kush: The Napatan and Meroitic Empires* (London 1996)

Meroë excavations and political context at the time of discovery

C. Breasted, *Pioneer to the Past: The Story of James Henry Breasted, Archaeologist* (Chicago 2009)

W. Churchill, *The River War: An Historical Account of the Reconquest of the Soudan* (London 1899)

A. H. Sayce, *Reminiscences* (London 1923)

L. Török, *Meroë City, an Ancient African Capital: John Garstang's Excavations in the Sudan* (London 1997)

Garstang's field notes, correspondence and the original photographs of the Meroë expedition are kept in The Garstang Museum of Archaeology, School of Archaeology, Classics & Egyptology, University of Liverpool: http://www.liv.ac.uk/archaeology-classics-and-egyptology/garstang-museum/

More material related to the story of the Meroë Head is on display at the British Museum in galleries 65 (Sudan, Egypt and Nubia) and 70 (The Roman Empire). This includes portraits of Augustus and members of his family and objects from Meroë, among them further finds from Garstang's excavations.

The British Museum's collection online

To explore the British Museum's collection online, visit: britishmuseum.org/research/search_the_collection_database.aspx

Author's acknowledgements

It is a great pleasure to thank the following colleagues at the British Museum and other institutions for their support in preparing this manuscript: Janet Ambers, Philip Fletcher, Marilyn Hockey, Judith Swaddling, Emma Poulter, Gabriele Rasbach (Römisch-Germanische Kommission, Frankfurt a. M.), Alex Reid, Libby Strudwick, Alex Truscott, Derek Welsby and Patricia Winker (formerly at the Garstang Museum and Archive, Liverpool). I am particularly grateful to Kevin Lovelock for his superb new photographs of the Meroë Head, and to Kate Morton, who provided the excellent maps and illustrations.

Much of the scientific analysis of the bronze head is based on research by my former British Museum colleague Paul Craddock.

Any book is based on the work of numerous others, and I apologize if the format of this series, without a full scholarly apparatus, does not allow me to acknowledge properly where I have been led by the research of so many bright experts.

Picture credits

Every effort has been made to trace the copyright holders of the images reproduced in this book. All British Museum photographs are © The Trustees of the British Museum.

Fig.

2   Museo della civiltà Romana; Sovraintendenza ai Beni Culturali di Roma Capitale

3–8   The Garstang Museum of Archaeology, School of Archaeology, Classics & Egyptology, University of Liverpool, UK

9   Mary Evans Picture Library

10   Illustration by Kate Morton; © The Trustees of the British Museum

11   Guillemette Andreu-Lanoë

12   Map by Kate Morton; © The Trustees of the British Museum

13   Illustrations by Kate Morton, based on the original watercolours by Horst Schliephack; © The Trustees of the British Museum

14   The Garstang Museum of Archaeology, School of Archaeology, Classics & Egyptology, University of Liverpool, UK

16   Vatican Museums, Rome; photo © B&Y Photography / Alamy

17   Museo Nazionale Romano, Palazzo Massimo alle Terme; photo: akg-images

18   Map by Kate Morton; © The Trustees of the British Museum

19a   Musei Capitolini, Rome; photo © Araldo de Luca/Corbis

19b   Musei Capitolini, Rome; photo: Cologne Digital Archaeology Laboratory, University of Cologne

19c   Musée du Louvre, Paris; photo © RMN-Grand Palais (musée du Louvre) / Hervé Lewandowski

19d   Musée du Louvre, Paris; photo © RMN-Grand Palais (musée du Louvre) / Hervé Lewandowski